Love

Letters

Of

Great

Men

Love

Letters

Of

Great

Men

Pacific Publishing Studio

Table of Contents

Arout Voltaire

Henry von Kleist

Woodrow Wilson

Sullivan Ballou

Edgar Allen Poe

Alexander Hamilton

If a picture which is but a mute representation of an object can give such pleasure, what cannot letters inspire? They have souls; they can speak. They have in them all that force which expresses the transport of the heart; they have all the fire of our passions....

Abigail Adams
To John Adams
December 23, 1782

My Dearest Friend,

...should I draw you the picture of my heart it would be what I hope you would still love though it contained nothing new. The early possession you obtained there, and the absolute power you have obtained over it, leaves not the smallest space unoccupied.

I look back to the early days of our acquaintance and friendship as to the days of love and innocence, and, with an indescribable pleasure, I have seen near a score of years roll over our heads with an affection heightened and improved by time, nor have the dreary years of absence in the smallest degree effaced from my mind the image of the dear untitled man to whom I gave my heart.

Algernon Charles Swinburne
"Love And Sleep"

Lying asleep between the strokes of night
I saw my love lean over my sad bed,
Pale as the duskiest lily's leaf or head,
Smooth-skinned and dark, with bare throat made to bite,
Too wan for blushing and too warm for white,
But perfect-coloured without white or red.

And her lips opened amorously, and said—
I wist not what, saving one word—Delight.

And all her face was honey to my mouth,
And all her body pasture to mine eyes;
The long lithe arms and hotter hands than fire
The quivering flanks, hair smelling of the south,
The bright light feet, the splendid supple thighs
And glittering eyelids of my soul's desire.

Alexander Pope
To Teresa Blount
August 7, 1716

Madam,

I have so much esteem for you and so much of the other thing that were I a handsome fellow, I should do you a vast deal of good; but as it is, all I am good for is to write a civil letter or to make a fine speech.

The truth is that considering how often and how openly I have declared love to you, I am astonished (and a little affronted) that you have not forbid my correspondence and directly said, 'See my face no more.'

It is not enough, Madam, for your reputation, that you keep your hands pure from the strain of such ink as might be shed to gratify a male correspondent; Alas! While your heart consents to encourage him in this lewd liberty of writing, you are not, indeed you are not, what you would so fain have me think you, a prude! I am vain enough to conclude (like most young fellows) that a fine lady's silence is consent, and I write on.

But in order to be as innocent as possible in this epistle, I'll tell you news. You have asked me news a thousand times at the first word you spoke to me, which some would interpret as if you expected nothing better from my lips.

And truly is it not a sign two lovers are together when they can be so impertinent as to inquire what the world does? All I mean by this is that either you or I cannot be in love with the other; I leave you to guess which of the two is that stupid and insensible creature, so blind to the others excellencies and charms...

Alexander Pope

George Farquar
To Anne Oldfield
Sunday 1699

Anne,

...I came, I saw, and was conquered; never had man more to say, yet can I say nothing; where others go to save their souls, there have I lost mine. But I hope that divinity which has the justest title to its service has received it; but I will endeavor to suspend these raptures for a moment and talk calmly.

Nothing on earth, madam, can charm beyond your wit but your beauty. After this, not to love you would proclaim me a fool; and to say I did when I thought otherwise, would pronounce me a knave; if anybody called me either, I should resent it; and if you but think me either, I shall break my heart.

You have already, madam, seen enough of me to create a liking or an aversion; your sense is above your sex, then let your proceeding be so likewise, and tell me plainly what I have to hope for. Were I to consult my merits, my humility would chide any shadow of hope. But after a sight of such a face whose whole composition is a smile of good nature, why should I be so unjust as to suspect you of cruelty?

Let me either live in London and be happy or retire again to my desert to check my vanity that drew me thence; but let me beg you to receive my sentence from your own mouth, that I may hear you speak and see you look at the same time; then, let me be unfortunate if I can.

If you are not the lady in mourning that sat upon my right hand at church, you may go to the devil, for I'm sure you're a witch.

George

Michael Faraday
To Sarah Barnard

The Royal Institution
December 1820,

My Dear Sarah,

It is astonishing how much the state of the body influences the powers of the mind.

I have been thinking all the morning of the very delightful and interesting letter I would send you this evening. And now I am so tired, and yet have so much to do, that my thoughts are quite giddy and run round your image without any power of themselves to stop and admire it.

I want to say a thousand kind and, believe me, heartfelt things to you but am not master of words fit for the purpose. And still, as I ponder and think on you, chlorides, trials, oil, Davy, steel, miscellanea, mercury, and fifty other professional fancies swim before and drive me further and further into the quandary of stupidness.

From your affectionate,
Michael

Oscar Wilde
To his wife, Constance
December 16, 1884

Dear Beloved,

Here am I, and you at the Antipodes. O, execrable facts that keep our lips from kissing though our souls are one.

What can I tell you by letter? Alas! Nothing that I would tell you; the messages of the gods to each other travel not by pen and ink; and indeed your bodily presence here would not make you more real. For I feel your fingers in my hair and your cheek brushing mine. The air is full of the music of your voice; my soul and body seem no longer mine—but mingled in some exquisite ecstasy with yours.

I feel incomplete without you.

Ever and ever yours, Oscar

P.S. Here I stay till Sunday.

Thomas Hood
To his wife

My own dearest and best,

We parted manfully and womanfully as we ought. I drank
only half a bottle of the Rhine wine and only the half of that,
ere I fell asleep on the sofa—which lasted two hours.

It was the reaction for your going that tired me more than I
cared to show. Then I drank the other half, and as that did
not do, I went and retraced our walk in the park and sat down
in the same seat and felt happier and better. Have you not a
romantic old husband?

Thomas Woodrow Wilson
To his wife, Ellen Axson Wilson
May 9, 1886

Ellen,

I've been reckoning up, in a tumultuous sort of way, the value of my little wife to me. I can't state the result—there are no terms of value in which it can be stated—but perhaps I can give you some ideas of what its proportions would be if it were stated.

She has taken all real pain out of my life. Her wonderful loving sympathy exalts even my occasional moods of despondency into a sort of hallowed sadness out of which I come stronger and better.

She has given to my ambitions a meaning, an assurance, and a purity, which they have never had before. With her by my side, ardently devoted to me and to my cause, understanding all my thoughts and all my aims.

I feel that I can make the utmost of every power I possess. She had brought into my life the sunshine, which was needed to keep it from growing stale and morbid. That has steadily been bringing back into my spirits their old gladness and boyhood, their old delight in play and laughter, that sweetest sunshine of deep womanly love, unfailing gentle patience— even happy spirits and spontaneous mirth that is the purest, swiftest tonic to a spirit prone to fret and apt to flag.

She has given me that perfect rest of heart and mind, of whose existence I had never so much as dreamed before she came to me—which springs out of assured oneness of hope and sympathy—and which, for me, means life and success.

Above all, she has given me herself to live for! Her arms are able to hold me up against the world; her eyes are able to charm away every care; her words are my solace and inspiration—and all because her love is my life.

Thomas

Amy Lowell
"Carrefour"

O you, Who came upon me once
Stretched under apple-trees just after bathing,
Why did you not strangle me before speaking
Rather than fill me with the wild honey of your words
And then leave me to the mercy
Of the forest bees?

William Congreve
To Arabella Hunt
1690

Dear Madam,

Not believe that I love you? You cannot pretend to be so incredulous. If you do not believe my tongue, consult my eyes, consult your own. You will find by yours that they have charms—by mine, that I have a heart which feels them.

Recall to mind what happened last night. That, at least, was a love's kiss. Its eagerness, its fierceness, its warmth expressed the God its parent. But oh! Its sweetness and its melting softness expressed him more. With trembling in my limbs and fevers in my soul, I ravished it. Convulsions, pantings, murmurings showed the mighty disorder within me: the mighty disorder increased by it.

For those dear lips shot, through my heart and through my bleeding vitals, delicious poison and an avoidless yet a charming ruin.

What cannot a day produce? The night before I thought myself a happy man, in want of nothing, and in fairest expectation of fortune, approved of by men of wit and applauded by others. Pleased, nay charmed with my friends, my then dearest friends, sensible of every delicate pleasure, and in their turn possessing all.

But love, almighty love, seems in a moment to have removed me to a prodigious distance from every object but you alone. In the midst of crowds, I remain in solitude. Nothing but you can lay hold of my mind, and that can lay hold of nothing but you. I appear transported to some foreign desert with you— oh, that I were really thus transported—where, abundantly supplied with everything in thee, I might live out an age of uninterrupted ecstasy.

The scene of the world's great stage seems suddenly and sadly changed. Unlovely objects are all around me, excepting thee; the charms of all the world appear to be translated to thee. Thus, in this said but oh, too pleasing state, my soul can fix upon nothing but thee. Thee it contemplates, admires, adores, nay depends on, trusts on you alone.

If you and hope forsake it, despair and endless attend it.

William

Johann Wolfgang von Goethe
To Charlotte von Stein

Charlotte,

My letters will have shown you how lovely I am. I don't dine at Court, I see few people, and take my walks alone. And at every beautiful spot I wish you were there.

I can't help loving you more than is good for me; I shall feel all the happier when I see you again. I am always conscious of my nearness to you; your presence never leaves me. In you I have a measure for every woman, for everyone; in your love a measure for all that is to be. Not in the sense that the rest of the world seems obscure tome. On the contrary, your love makes it clear; I see quite clearly what men are like and what they plan, wish, do, and enjoy. I don't grudge them what they have, and comparing is a secret joy to me, possessing as I do such an imperishable treasure.

You, in your household, must feel as I often do in my affairs; we often don't notice objects simply because we don't choose to look at them, but things acquire an interest as soon as we see clearly the way they are related to each other. For we always like to join in, and the good man takes pleasure in arranging, putting in order, and furthering the right and its peaceful rule.

Adieu, you whom I love a thousand times.

Johann

Victor Hugo
To Adele Foucher
1821- 1822

My dearest,

When two souls, which have sought each other for however long in the throng, have finally found each other ...a union, fiery and pure as they themselves are... begins on earth and continues forever in heaven.

This union is love, true love, ... a religion which deifies the loved one, whose life comes from devotion and passion, and for which the greatest sacrifices are the sweetest delights.

This is the love which you inspire in me... Your soul is made to love with the purity and passion of angels; but perhaps it can only love another angel, in which case I must tremble with apprehension.

Yours forever, Victor Hugo

March 15, 1822

Dearest,

After the two delightful evenings spent yesterday and the day before, I shall certainly not go out tonight, but will sit here at home and write to you. Besides, my Adele, my adorable and adored Adele, what have I not to tell you? O, God! For two days, I have been asking myself every moment if such happiness is not a dream. It seems to me that what I feel is not of earth. I cannot yet comprehend this cloudless heaven.

You do not yet know, Adele, to what I had resigned myself. Alas, do I know it myself? Because I was weak, I fancied I was calm; because I was preparing myself for all the mad follies of despair, I thought I was courageous and resigned. Ah! let me cast myself humbly at your feet; you, who are so grand, so tender and strong! I had been thinking that the utmost limit of my devotion could only be the sacrifice of my life; but you, my generous love, were ready to sacrifice for me the repose of yours.

...You have been privileged to receive every gift from nature; you have both fortitude and tears. Oh, Adele, do not mistake these words for blind enthusiasm—enthusiasm for you has lasted all my life and increased day by day. My whole soul is yours. If my entire existence had not been yours, the harmony of my being would have been lost, and I must have died—died inevitably.

These were my meditations, Adele, when the letter that was to bring me hope of else despair arrived. If you love me, you know what must have been my joy. What I know you may have felt, I will not describe.

My Adele, why is there no word for this but joy? Is it because there is no power in human speech to express such happiness?

The sudden bound from mournful resignation to infinite felicity seemed to upset me. Even now I am still beside myself, and sometimes I tremble lest I should suddenly awaken from this dream divine.

Oh, now you are mine! At last you are mine! Soon—in a few months, perhaps, my angel will sleep in my arms, will awaken in my arms, will live there. All your thoughts at all moments, all your looks will be for me; all my thoughts, all my moments, all my looks, will be for you! My Adele!

Adieu, my angel, my beloved Adele! Adieu! I will kiss your hair and go to bed. Still I am far from you, but I can dream of you. Soon perhaps you will be at my side. Adieu; pardon the delirium of your husband who embraces you and who adores you, both for this life and another.

Victor

Juliette Drouet
To Victor Hugo
1835

If only I were a clever woman, I could describe to you my gorgeous bird, how you unite in yourself the beauties of form, plumage, and song!

I would tell you that you are the greatest marvel of all ages, and I should only be speaking the simple truth. But to put all this into suitable words, my superb one, I should require a voice far more harmonious than that which is bestowed upon my species—for I am the humble owl that you mocked at only lately, therefore, it cannot be.

I will not tell you to what degree you are dazzling and to the birds of sweet song who, as you know, are none the less beautiful and appreciative.

I am content to delegate to them the duty of watching, listening and admiring, while to myself I reserve the right of loving; this may be less attractive to the ear, but it is sweeter far to the heart.

I love you, I love you. My Victor; I cannot reiterate it too often; I can never express it as much as I feel it.

I recognize you in all the beauty that surrounds me in form, in color, in perfume, in harmonious sound: all of these mean you to me. You are superior to all. I see and admire—you are all!

You are not only the solar spectrum with the seven luminous colors, but the sun himself, that illumines, warms, and revivifies! This is what you are, and I am the lowly woman that adores you.

Juliette

Honore de Balzac
To Evelina Hanska

October 6, 1833

Evelina,

Our love will bloom always fairer, fresher, more gracious because it is a true love and because genuine love is ever increasing.

It is a beautiful plant growing from year to year in the heart, ever extending its palms and branches, doubling every season its glorious clusters and perfumes. And my dear life, tell me, repeat to me always that nothing will bruise its bark or its delicate leaves, that it will grow larger in both our hearts, loved, free, watched over like a life within our life...

June 19, 1836

My beloved angel,

I am nearly mad about you, as much as one can be mad: I cannot bring together two ideas that you do not interpose yourself between them.

I can no longer think of anything but you. In spite of myself, my imagination carries me to you. I grasp you, I kiss you, I caress you. A thousand of the most amorous caresses take possession of me.

As for my heart, there you will always be—very much so. I have a delicious sense of you there. But my God, what is to become of me if you have deprived me of my reason? This is a monomania—which, this morning, terrifies me.

I rise up every moment saying to myself, "Come, I am going there!" Then I sit down again, moved by the sense of my obligations. There is a frightful conflict. This is not life. I have never before been like that. You have devoured everything.

I feel foolish and happy as soon as I think of you. I whirl round in a delicious dream in which in one instant I live a thousand years. What a horrible situation!

Overcome with love, feeling love in every pore, living only for love, and seeing oneself consumed by griefs and caught in a thousand spiders' threads.

O, my darling Eva, you did not know it. I picked up your card. It is there before me, and I talk to you as if you were there. I see you as I did yesterday: beautiful, astonishingly beautiful.

Yesterday, during the whole evening I said to myself, "she is mine!" Ah! The angels are not as happy in Paradise as I was yesterday!

Balzac

Charlotte Bronte
To Professor Constantin Heger

January 8, 1845

Monsieur,

The poor have not need of much to sustain them—they ask only for the crumbs that fall from the rich man's table. But if they are refused the crumbs, they die of hunger.

Nor do I, either, need much affection from those I love. I should not know what to do with a friendship entire and complete—I am not used to it. But you showed me of yore a little interest, when I was your pupil in Brussels, and I hold on to the maintenance of that little interest.

I hold on to it as I would hold on to life.

Gaius Plinius Caecilius Secundus
"Pliny the Younger"
c. A.D. 100

You say that you are feeling my absence very much, and your only comfort when I am not there is to hold my writings in your hand and often put them in my place by your side.

I like to think that you miss me and find relief in this sort of consolation. I, too, am always reading your letters and returning to them again and again, as if they were new to me. But this only fans the fire of my longing for you.

If your letters are so dear to me, you can imagine how I delight in your company; do write as often as you can— although you give me pleasure mingled with pain.

Matthew Arnold
"Longing"

Come to me in my dreams, and then
By day I shall be well again!
For so the night will more than pay
The hopeless longing of the day.

Come, as thou cam'st a thousand times,
A messenger from radiant climes,
And smile on thy new world, and be
As kind to others as to me!

Or, as thou never cam'st in sooth,
Come now, and let me dream it truth,
And part my hair, and kiss my brow,
And say, My love why sufferest thou?

Come to me in my dreams, and then
By day I shall be well again!
For so the night will more than pay
The hopeless longing of the day.

Frances Anne Kemble
To James Sheridan Knowles
London, December 1842

Having loved you well enough to give you my life when it was best worth giving—having made you the center of all my hopes of earthly happiness—having never loved any human being as I have loved you, you can never be to me like any other human being. And it is utterly impossible that I should ever regard you with indifference.

My whole existence—having once had you for its sole object and all its thoughts, hopes, affections having, in their full harvest, been yours—it is utterly impossible that I should ever forget this; that I should ever forget that you were once my lover and are my husband and the father of my children.

I cannot behold you without emotion; my heart still answers to your voice—my blood in my veins to your footsteps.

From Ludwig Van Beethoven
To Immortal Beloved

My Immortal Beloved,

Though still in bed, my thoughts go out to you, my Immortal Beloved, now and then joyfully, then sadly, waiting to learn whether or not fate will hear us—I can live only wholly with you or not at all. Yes, I am resolved to wander so long away from you until I can fly to your arms and say that I am really at home with you, and can send my soul enwrapped in you into the land of spirits. Yes, unhappily it must be so—You will be the more contained since you know my fidelity to you. No one else can ever possess my heart— never—never.

Oh God, why must one be parted from one whom one so loves. And yet my life in Vienna is now a wretched life—Your love makes me at once the happiest and the unhappiest of men. At my age I need a steady, quiet life. Can that be so in our connection? My angel, I have just been told that the mail coach goes every day—therefore I must close at once so that you may receive the letter at once. Be calm. Only by a calm consideration of our existence can we achieve our purpose to live together. Be calm. Love me—today—yesterday—what tearful longings for you—you—you—my life—my all— farewell. Oh continue to love me—never misjudge the most faithful heart of your beloved.

Ever thine
Ever mine
Ever ours

Napolean Bonaparte
To Josephine Beauharnais
1795-1797

Paris, December 1795

Josephine,

I wake filled with thoughts of you. Your portrait and the intoxicating evening which we spent yesterday have left my senses in turmoil. Sweet, incomparable Josephine, what a strange effect you have on my heart! Are you angry? Do I see you looking sad? Are you worried?...

My soul aches with sorrow and there can be no rest for you, lover; but is there still more in store for me when, yielding to the profound feelings which overwhelm me, I draw from your lips, from your heart a love which consumes me with fire? Ah! It was last night that I fully realized how false an image of you your portrait gives!

You are leaving at noon; I shall see you in three hours.

Until then, mio dolce amor, a thousand kisses; but give me none in return, for they set my blood on fire.

Napolean

Spring 1797

To Josephine,

I love you no longer; on the contrary, I detest you. You are a wretch, truly perverse, truly stupid, a real Cinderella. You never write to me at all, you do not love your husband; you know the pleasure that your letters give him, yet you cannot even manage to write him half a dozen lines, dashed off in a moment!

What then do you do all day, Madame? What business is so vital that it robs you of the time to write to your faithful lover? What attachment can be stifling and pushing aside the love, the tender and constant love which you promised him? Who can this wonderful new lover be who takes up your every moment, rules your days and prevents you from devoting your attention to your husband?

Beware, Josephine, one fine night the doors will be broken down and there I shall be. In truth, I am worried, my love, to have no news from you. Write me a four page letter instantly made up from those delightful words which fill my heart with emotion and joy. I hope to hold you in my arms before long, when I shall lavish upon you a million kisses, burning as the equatorial sun.

Napolean

Katherine Mansfield
To John Middleton Murry
1917-1918

Saturday Night
May 19, 1917

My darling,

Do not imagine, because you find these lines in your journal, that I have been trespassing. You know I have not—and where else shall I leave a love letter? For I long to write you a love-letter tonight.

You are all about me—I seem to breathe you, hear you, feel you in me and of me.

What am I doing here? You are away. I have seen you in the train, at the station, driving up, sitting in the lamplight, talking, greeting people, washing your hands... And I am here—in your tent—sitting at your table.

There are some wall-flower petals on the table and a dead match, a blue pencil, and a Magdeburgische Zeitung. I am just as much at home as they.

When dusk came, flowing up the silent garden, lapping against the blind windows, my first and last terror started up. I was making some coffee in the kitchen. It was so violent, so dreadful I put down the coffee pot and simply ran away—ran, ran out of the studio and up the street with my bag under one arm and a block of writing paper and a pen under the other. I felt that if I could get here and find Mrs. F I should be safe.

I found her and I lighted your gas, wound up your clock, drew your curtains, and embraced your black overcoat before I sat down—frightened no longer.

Do not be angry with me, Bogey. Ca a ete plus fort que moi .... That is why I am here.

When you came to tea this afternoon you took a brioche, broke it in half, and padded the inside doughy bit with two fingers. You always do that with a bun, or roll, or a piece of bread. It is your way—your head a little on one side the while.

When you opened your suitcase, I saw your old Feltie, and a French book, and a comb all higgledy-piggledy. 'Tig, I've only got three handkerchiefs.' Why should that memory be so sweet to me?...

Last night, there was a moment before you got into bed. You stood, quite naked, bending forward a little, talking. It was only for an instant. I saw you—I loved you so, loved your body with such tenderness. Ah, my dear!

And I am not thinking of passion. No, of that other thing that makes me feel that every inch of you is so precious to me—your soft shoulders, your creamy warm skin, your ears cold like shells are cold, your long legs and your feet that I love to clasp with my feet—the feeling of your belly and your thin young back. Just below that bone that sticks out at the back of your neck you have a little mole.

It is partly because we are young that I feel this tenderness. I love your mouth. I could not bear that it should be touched even by a cold wind if I were the Lord.

We two, you know, have everything before us, and we shall do very great things. I have perfect faith in us, and so perfect is my love for you that I am, as it were, still silent to my very soul.

I want nobody but you for my lover and my friend, and to nobody but you shall I be faithful.

I am yours forever.

Tig

January 27, 1918

My love for you tonight is so deep and tender that it seems to be outside myself as well. I am fast shut up like a little lake in the embrace of some big mountains. If you were to climb up the mountains, you would see me down below—deep and shining and quite fathomless, my dear. You might drop your heart into me and you'd never hear it touch bottom.

I love you. I love you. Goodnight.

Oh Bogey, what it is to love like this!

Mark Twain
To his future wife, Olivia Langdon

May 12, 1869

Out of the depths of my happy heart wells a great tide of love and prayer for this priceless treasure that is confided to my life-long keeping.

You cannot see its intangible waves as they flow towards you, darling. But in these lines you will hear, as it were, the distant beating of the surf.

James Joyce
To Nora Barnacle
15 August, 1904

My dear Nora,

It has just struck me. I came in at half past eleven. Since then I have been sitting in an easy chair like a fool. I could do nothing. I hear nothing but your voice. I am like a fool hearing you call me 'Dear.' I offended two men today by leaving them coolly. I wanted to hear your voice, not theirs.

When I am with you, I leave aside my contemptuous, suspicious nature. I wish I felt your head on my shoulder. I think I will go to bed.

I have been a half-hour writing this thing. Will you write something to me? I hope you will. How am I to sign myself? I won't sign anything at all because I don't know what to sign myself.

James

Tsarina Alexandra
To Tsar Nicholas II of Russia
December 30, 1915

Off you go again alone, and it's with a very heavy heart I part from you. No more kisses and tender caresses forever so long. I want to bury myself in you, hold you tight in my arms, make you feel the intense love of mine.

You are my very life Sweetheart, and every separation gives such endless heartache...

Goodbye my Angel, Husband of my heart—I envy my flowers that will accompany you. I press you tightly to my breast, kiss every sweet place with tender love...

God bless and protect you, guard you from all harm, guide you safely and firmly into the new year. May it bring glory and sure peace, and the reward for all this war has cost you.

I gently press my lips to yours and try to forget everything. Gazing into your lovely eyes, I lay on your precious breast, resting my tired head upon it still. This morning I tried to gain calm and strength for the separation.

Goodbye wee one, Lovebird, Sunshine, Huzy, mine Own!

Franz Kafka
To Fraulein Felice Bauer
November 11, 1912

Fräulein Felice!

I am now going to ask you a favor which sounds quite crazy and which I should regard as such, were I the one to receive the letter. It is also the very greatest test that even the kindest person could be put to. Well, this is it:

Write to me only once a week so that your letter arrives on Sunday—for I cannot endure your daily letters; I am incapable of enduring them. For instance, I answer one of your letters, then lie in bed in apparent calm, but my heart beats through my entire body and is conscious only of you. I belong to you; there is really no other way of expressing it and that is not strong enough. But for this very reason, I don't want to know what you are wearing; it confuses me so much that I cannot deal with life; and that's why I don't want to know that you are fond of me.

If I did, how could I, fool that I am, go on sitting in my office, or here at home, instead of leaping onto a train with my eyes shut and opening them only when I am with you? Oh, there is a sad, sad reason for not doing so. To make it short: My health is only just good enough for myself alone, not good enough for marriage, let alone fatherhood. Yet when I read your letter, I feel I could overlook even what cannot possibly be overlooked.

If only I had your answer now! And how horribly I torment you and how I compel you, in the stillness of your room, to read this letter, as nasty a letter as has ever lain on your desk! Honestly, it strikes me sometimes that I prey like a spectre on your felicitous name! If only I had mailed Saturday's letter, in which I implored you never to write to me again and in which I gave a similar promise. Oh God, what prevented me from sending that letter? All would be well.

But is a peaceful solution possible now? Would it help if we wrote to each other only once a week? No, if my suffering could be cured by such means it would not be serious. And already I foresee that I shan't be able to endure even the Sunday letters. And so, to compensate for Saturday's lost opportunity, I ask you with what energy remains to me at the end of this letter: If we value our lives, let us abandon it all.

Franz

William Shakespeare
"Shall I Compare Thee To A Summers Day?"

Shall I compare thee to a summersday?
Thou art more lovely and more temperate:
Rough winds do shake the darling buds of May,
And summer's lease hath all too short a day:
Sometime too hot the eye of heaven shines,
And often is his gold complexion dimm'd;
And every fair from fair sometime declines,
By chance, or nature's changing course untrimm'd:
But thy eternal summer shall not fade,
Nor loose possession of that fair thou ow'st;
Nor shall Death brag thou wand'rest in his shade,
When in eternal lines to time thou grow'st:
So long as men can breathe or eyes can see,
So long lives this, and this gives life to thee.

Rupert Brooke
To Noel Olivier
October 2, 1911

I have a thousand images of you in an hour; all different and all coming back to the same... And we love. And we've got the most amazing secrets and understandings. Noel, whom I love, who is so beautiful and wonderful; I think of you eating omlette on the ground. I think of you once against a sky line and on the hill that Sunday morning.

And that night was wonderfullest of all. The light and the shadow and quietness and the rain and the wood. And you; you are so beautiful and wonderful that I daren't write to you... And kinder than God.

Your arms and lips and hair and shoulders and voice—you.

Robert Browning
To Elizabeth Barrett
January 10, 1846

Dearest,

Do you know, when you have told me to think of you, I have
been feeling ashamed of thinking of you so much, of thinking
of only you—which is too much, perhaps. Shall I tell you? It
seems to me, to myself, that no man was ever before to any
woman what you are to me—the fullness must be in
proportion, you know, to the vacancy...and only I know what
was behind—the long wilderness without the blossoming
rose...and the capacity for happiness, like a black gaping hole,
before this silver flooding. Is it wonderful that I should stand
as in a dream and disbelieve—not you—but my own fate?

Was ever anyone taken suddenly from a lampless dungeon
and placed upon the pinnacle of a mountain, without the
head turning round and the heart turning faint, as mine does?
And you love me more, you say? Shall I thank you or God?
Both, indeed, and there is no possible return from me to
either of you! I thank you as the unworthy may... and as we all
thank God.

How shall I ever prove what my heart is to you? How will you
ever see it as I feel it? I ask myself in vain. Have so much faith
in me, my only beloved, as to use me simply for your own
advantage and happiness and to your own ends without a
thought of any others. That is all I could ask you without any
disquiet as to the granting of it.

May God bless you! Your B.A.

Robert Browning

Elizabeth Barrett Browing
To Robert Browning

And now listen to me in turn. You have touched me more profoundly than I thought even you could have touched me—my heart was full when you came here today. Henceforward, I am yours for everything....

Elizabeth Barrett Browning
"How Do I Love Thee?"

How do I love thee? Let me count the ways.
I love thee to the depth and breadth and height
My soul can reach, when feeling out of sight
For the ends of Being and ideal Grace.
I love thee to the level of every day's
Most quiet need, by sun and candlelight.
I love thee freely, as men strive for Right;
I love thee purely, as they turn from Praise.
I love with a passion put to use
In my old griefs, and with my childhood's faith.
I love thee with a love I seemed to lose
With my lost saints, I love thee with the breath,
Smiles, tears, of all my life! and, if God choose,
I shall but love thee better after death.

Elizabeth Barret Browning
"Bianca Among The Nightingales"

We paled with love, we shook with love,
We kissed so close we could not vow;
Till Giulio whispered, `Sweet, above
God's Ever guarantees this Now.'
And through his words the nightingales
Drove straight and full their long clear call,
Like arrows through heroic mails,
And love was awful in it all.
The nightingales, the nightingales.

O cold white moonlight of the north,
Refresh these pulses, quench this hell!
O coverture of death drawn forth
Across this garden-chamber... well!
But what have nightingales to do
In gloomy England, called the free.
(Yes, free to die in!...) when we two
Are sundered, singing still to me?
And still they sing, the nightingales.

I think I hear him, how he cried
`My own soul's life' between their notes.
Each man has but one soul supplied,
And that's immortal. Though his throat's
On fire with passion now, to her
He can't say what to me he said!
And yet he moves her, they aver.
The nightingales sing through my head.
The nightingales, the nightingales.

Jane Baillie Welsh
To Thomas Carlyle
October 3, 1826

...it is so easy a thing for you to lift me to Seventh Heaven! My soul was darker than midnight when your pen said, "let there be light." And there was light as at the bidding of the Word...

When I read in your looks and words that you love me, I feel it in the deepest part of my soul; and then I care not one straw for the whole Universe beside...

Robert Burdette
To his future wife, Clara Baker
April 25, 1898

And when I have reasoned it all out and set metes and
bounds for your love that it may not pass, lo, a letter from
Clara. And in one sweet, ardent, pure, Edenic page, her love
overrides my boundaries as the sea sweeps over rocks and
sands alike, crushes my barriers into dust—out of which they
were built, overwhelms me with its beauty, bewilders me with
its sweetness, charms me with its purity, and loses me in its
great shoreless immensity.

Lord Byron
To Lady Caroline Lamb
1812

April 7, 1812

Caroline,

I never supposed you artful. We are all selfish; nature did that for us. But even when you attempt deceit occasionally, you cannot maintain it, which is all the better.

Want of success will curb the tendency. Every word you utter, every line you write proves you to be either sincere or a fool. Now as I know you are one, I must believe you the other.

I never knew a woman with greater or more pleasing talents, general as in a woman they should be, something of everything, and too much of nothing. But these are unfortunately coupled with a total want of common conduct. For instance, the note to your page, do you suppose I delivered it? Or did you mean that I should? I did not of course.

Then your heart—my poor Caro, what a little volcano that pours lava through your veins. And yet, I cannot wish it a bit colder, to make a marble slab of, as you sometimes see (to understand my foolish metaphor), brought in vases and see from Vesuvius, when hardened after an eruption.

To drop my detertable tropes and figures—you know I have always thought you the cleverest most agreeable, absurd,

LOVE LETTERS OF GREAT MEN

amiable, perplexing, dangerous, fascinating little being that lives now or ought to have lived 2000 years ago. I won't talk to you of beauty; I am no judge.

But our beauties cease to be so when near you, and therefore, you have either some or something better. And now, Caro, this non—sense is the first and last compliment (if it be such) I even paid you. You have often reproached me as wanting in that respect, but others will make up the deficiency ...

All that you so often say, I feel. Can more be said or felt? This same prudence is tiresome enough, but one must maintain it, or what can we do to be saved?

Keep to it.

August 1812

My dearest Caroline,

If tears, which you saw and know I am not apt to shed, if the agitation in which I parted from you, agitation which you must have perceived through the whole of this most nervous nervous affair, did not commence till the moment of leaving you approached. If all that I have said and done, and am still but too ready to say and do, have not sufficiently proved what my real feelings are and must be ever towards you, my love, I have no other proof to offer.

God knows I wish you happy and when I quit you, or rather when you, from a sense of duty to your husband and mother, quit me, you shall acknowledge the truth of what I again promise and vow: that no other, in word or deed, shall ever hold the place in my affection which is and shall be most sacred to you, till I am nothing.

I never knew till that moment, the madness of—my dearest and most beloved friend—I cannot express myself—this is no time for words—but I shall have a pride, a melancholy pleasure in suffering what you yourself can hardly conceive— for you do not know Me. I am now about to go out with a heavy heart, because my appearing this evening will stop any absurd story which the events of today might give rise to—

Do you think now that I am cold and stern and artful? Will even others think so, will your mother even—that mother to whom we must indeed sacrifice much, much more on my part than she shall ever know or can imagine?

"Promises not to love you," ah, Caroline, it is past promising— but shall attribute all concessions to the proper motive—and never cease to feel all that you have already witnessed and more than can ever be known but to my own heart—perhaps to yours. May God protect, forgive, and bless you—ever and even more than ever.

your most attached,

Byron

P.S. These taunts which have driven you to this, my dearest Caroline, were it not for your mother and the kindness of all your connections—is there anything on earth or heaven that would have made me so happy as to have made you mine long ago? And not less now than then, but more than ever at this time—you know I would, with pleasure, give up all here and all beyond the grave for you.

And in refraining from this, must my motives be misunderstood? I care not who knows this—what use is made of it. It is you and to you only that they owe yourself. I was and am yours—freely and most entirely—to obey, to honor, love—and fly with you when, where, and how you yourself might and may determine.

From Lord Byron
To future wife, Annabella Milbanke

November 16, 1814

My Heart,

We are thus far separated—but after all, one mile is as bad as a thousand—which is a great consolation to one who must travel six hundred before he meets you again. If it will give you any satisfaction—I am as comfortless as a pilgrim with peas in his shoes and as cold as Charity, Chastity, or any other Virtue.

Lord Byron
To Teresa Guiccioli
August 25, 1819

My dearest Teresa,

I have read this book in your garden. My love, you were absent or else I could not have read it. It is a favorite book of yours and the writer was a friend of mine. You will not understand these English words, and others will not understand them—which is the reason I have not scrawled them in Italian. But you will recognize the handwriting of him who passionately loved you, and you will divine that, over a book which was yours, he could only think of love.

In that word, beautiful in all languages, but most so in yours—Amor mio—is comprised my existence here and hereafter. I feel I exist here, and I feel I shall exist hereafter— to what purpose you will decide. My destiny rests with you— and you are a woman, eighteen years of age. And two out of a convent.

I love you, and you love me—at least, you say so and act as if you did so, which last is a great consolation in all events.

But I more than love you and cannot cease to love you. Think of me, sometimes, when the Alps and ocean divide us—but they never will unless you wish it.

George

Jane Clairmont
To Lord Byron
1815

You bid me write short to you and I have much to say. You also bade me believe that it was a fancy which made me cherish an attachment for you. It cannot be a fancy since you have been for the last year the object upon which every solitary moment led me to muse.

I do not expect you to love me, I am not worthy of your love. I feel you are superior, yet much to my surprise, more to my happiness, you betrayed passions I had believed no longer alive in your bosom.

Shall I also have to ruefully experience the want of happiness? Shall I reject it when it is offered? I may appear to you imprudent, vicious; my opinions detestable, my theory depraved; but one thing, at least, time shall show you: that I love gently and with affection, that I am incapable of anything approaching the feeling of revenge or malice; I do assure you, your future will shall be mine, and everything you shall do or say, I shall not question.

Lord Randolph Churchill
To Jennie
August 1873

Jennie,

I cannot keep myself from writing any longer to you dearest, although I have not had any answer to either of my two letters. I suppose your mother does not allow you to write to me. Perhaps you have not got either of my letters...I am so dreadfully afraid that perhaps you may think I am forgetting you.

I can assure you, dearest Jeannette, you have not been out of my thoughts hardly for one minute since I left you Monday. I have written to my father everything—how much I love you, how much I long and pray and how much I would sacrifice, if it were necessary, to be married to you and to live ever after with you.

I shall get an answer Monday and whichever way it lies, I shall go to Cowes soon after and tell your mother everything. I am afraid she does not like me very much, from what I have heard...I would do anything she wished if she only would not oppose us. Dearest, if you are as fond of me as I am of you— nothing human could keep us long apart.

This last week has seemed an eternity to me. Oh, I would give my soul for another of those days we had together not long ago. Oh, if I could only get one line from you to reassure me, but I dare not ask you to do anything that your mother would disapprove of or has perhaps forbidden you to do. Sometimes I doubt, so I cannot help it, whether you really like me as you said at Cowes you did. If you do, I cannot fear for the future—though difficulties may lie in our way, only to be surmounted by patience.

Goodbye, dearest Jeannette, my first and only love...Believe me ever to be yours devotedly and lovingly,

Randolph S. Churchill

Edith Wharton
To W Morton Fullerton
June 8, 1908

There would have been the making of an accomplished flirt in me, because my lucidity shows me each move of the game—but that, in the same instant, a reaction of contempt makes me sweep all the counters off the board and cry out, "Take them all—I don't want to win—I want to lose everything to you!"

John Constable
To Maria Bicknell
East Bergholt

February 27, 1816

Maria Bicknell,

I received your letter, my ever dearest Maria, this morning. You know my anxious disposition too well not to be aware how much I feel at this time. At the distance we are from each other, every fear will obtrude itself on my mind. Let me hope that you are not really worse than your kindness. Your affection for me makes you say...I think...that no more molestation will arise to the recovery of your health, which I pray for beyond every other blessing under heaven.

Let us think only of the blessings that Providence may yet have in store for us and that we may yet possess. I am happy in love—an affection exceeding a thousand times my deserts, which has continued so many years and is yet undiminished. Never will I marry in this world if I marry not you. Truly can I say that for the seven years since I avowed my love for you, I have...foregone all company and the society of all females (except my own relations) for your sake.

I am still ready to make my sacrifice for you...I will submit to anything you may command me—but cease to respect, to love, and adore you—I never can or will. I must still think that we should have married long ago. We should have had many troubles—but we have yet had no joys and we could not have

LOVE LETTERS OF GREAT MEN

starved...Your friends have never been without a hope of parting us, and see what that has cost us both.

But no more. Believe me, my beloved and ever dearest Maria.

Most faithfully yours, John

From Duff Cooper
To his future wife, Diana
August 20, 1918

Darling, my darling. One line in haste to tell you that I love you more today than ever in my life before, that I never see beauty without thinking of you or scent happiness without thinking of you. You have fulfilled all my ambition, realized all my hopes, made all my dreams come true.

You have set a crown of roses on my youth and fortified me against the disaster of our days. Your courageous gaiety has inspired me with joy. Your tender faithfulness has been a rock of security and comfort. I have felt for you all kinds of love at once.

I have asked much of you and you have never failed me. You have intensified all colors, heightened all beauty, deepened all delight. I love you more than life, my beauty, my wonder.

Henry Constable
My Lady's Presence Makes the Roses Red

My lady's presence makes the roses red,
Because to see her lips they blush for shame.
The lily's leaves, for envy, pale became,
And her white hands in them this envy bred.
The marigold the leaves abroad doth spread,

Because the sun's and her power is the same.
The violet of purple colour came.
Dyed in the blood she made my heart to shed.
In brief: all flowers from her their virtue take;
From her sweet breath their sweet smells do proceed;

The living heat which her eyebeams doth make
Warmeth the ground and quickeneth the seed.
The rain, wherewith she watereth the flowers,
Falls from mine eyes, which she dissolves in showers.

Mary Wollstonecraft
To William Godwin
October 4, 1796

I would have liked to have dined with you today, after finishing your essay—that my eyes, and lips, I do not exactly mean my voice, might have told you that they had raised you in my esteem. What a cold word! I would say love—if you will promise not to dispute about its propriety, when I want to express an increasing affection—founded on a more intimate acquaintance with your heart and understanding.

I shall cork up all my kindness—yet the fine volatile essence may fly off in my walk. You know not how much tenderness for you may escape in a voluptuous sigh, should the air, as is often the case, give a pleasurable movement to the sensations that have been clustering round my heart, as I read this morning—reminding myself, every now and then, that the writer loved me.

Voluptuous is often expressive of a meaning I do not now intend to give, I would describe one of those moments, when the senses are exactly tuned by the ringing tenderness of the heart and according reason entices you to live in the present moment, regardless of the past or future. It is not rapture. It is sublime tranquility.

I have felt it in your arms—hush! Let not the light see, I was going to say hear it—these confessions should only be uttered—you know where, when the curtains are up—and all the world shut out—Ah me!

I wish I may find you at home when I carry this letter to drop it in the box—that I may drop a kiss with it into your heart, to be embalmed, till we meet, closer.

Pierre Curie
To Marie Sklodovska
August 10, 1894

Marie,

Nothing could have given me greater pleasure than to get news of you. The prospect of remaining two months without hearing about you had been extremely disagreeable to me; that is to say, your little note was more than welcome.

I hope you are laying up a stock of good air and that you will come back to us in October. As for me, I think I shall not go anywhere; I shall stay in the country where I spend the whole day in front of my open window or in the garden.

We have promised each other—haven't we—to be at least great friends? If you will only not change your mind! For there are no promises that are binding; such things cannot be ordered at will. It would be a fine thing, just the same, in which I hardly dare believe, to pass our lives near each other, hypnotized by our dreams: your patriotic dream, our humanitarian dream, and our scientific dream.

Of all those dreams the last is, I believe, the only legitimate one. I mean by that that we are powerless to change the social order and, even if we were not, we should not know what to do. In taking action, no matter in what direction, we should never be sure of not doing more harm than good by retarding some inevitable evolution. From the scientific point of view, on the contrary, we may hope to do something. The ground is solider here and any discovery that we may make, however small, will remain acquired knowledge.

See how it works out: it is agreed that we shall be great friends, but if you leave France in a year, it would be an altogether too Platonic friendship—that of two creatures who would never see each other again.

Wouldn't it be better for you to stay with me? I know that this question angers you and that you don't want to speak of it again—and then, too, I feel so thoroughly unworthy of you from every point of view.

I thought of asking your permission to meet you by chance in Fribourg. But you are staying there, unless I am mistaken, only one day. And on that day you will of course belong to our friends, the Kovalskis.

Believe me—your very devoted,
Pierre Curie

From Winston Churchill
To his wife, Clementine

January 23, 1935
My darling Clemmie,

In your letter from Madras, you wrote some words very dear to me about my having enriched your life. I cannot tell you what pleasure this gave me, because I always feel so overwhelmingly in your debt—if there can be accounts in love.... What it has been to me to live all these years in your heart and companionship—no phrases can convey.

Time passes swiftly, but is it not joyous to see how great and growing is the treasure we have gathered together amid the storms and stresses of so many eventful, and to millions, tragic and terrible years?

Your loving husband

Mary Wordsworth
To her husband, William Wordsworth
August 1, 1810

Oh My William!

It is not in my power to tell thee how I have been affected by this dearest of all letters. It was so unexpected—so new a thing to see the breathing of thy inmost heart upon paper that I was quite overpowered, and now that I sit down to answer thee in the loneliness and depth of that love—which unites us and which cannot be felt but by ourselves—I am so agitated and my eyes are so bedimmed that I scarcely know how to proceed...

Alfred de Musset
To Amantine Aurore Dudevant
1833-1834

1833

Dear Amantine,
I have something stupid and ridiculous to tell you. I am
foolishly writing to you, instead of having told you this, I do
not know why, when returning from that walk.

Tonight I shall be annoyed at having done so. You will laugh
in my face; will take me for a maker of phrases in all my
relations with you hitherto. You will show me the door and
you will think I am lying.

I am in love with you. I have been thus since the first day I
called on you.

Alfred de Musset

September 1, 1834
Dearest,

But let me have this letter, containing nothing but your love;
and tell me that you give me your lips, your hair, all that face

that I have possessed, and tell me that we embrace—you and I!

O God, O God, when I think of it, my throat closes, my sight is troubled, my knees fail. Ah, it is horrible to die, it is also horrible to love like this! What longing, what longing I have for you! I beg you to let me have the letter I ask. I am dying. Farewell.

Alfred de Musset

Christopher Marlowe
"The Passionate Shepherd to His Love"

Come live with me and be my Love,
And we will all the pleasures prove
That hills and valleys, dales and fields,
Or woods or steepy mountain yields.
And we will sit upon the rocks,
And see the shepherds feed their flocks
By shallow rivers, to whose falls
Melodious birds sing madrigals.
And I will make thee beds of roses
And a thousand fragrant posies;
A cap of flowers, and a kirtle
Embroidered all with leaves of myrtle;
A gown made of the finest wool
Which from our pretty lambs we pull;
Fair-lined slippers for the cold,
With buckles of the purest gold;
A belt of straw and ivy buds
With coral clasps and amber studs-
And if these pleasures may thee move,
Come live with me and by my Love.
The shepherd swains shall dance and sing
For thy delight each May morning-
If these delights thy mind may move,
Then live with me and be my Love.

Gustave Flaubert
To His wife Louise Colet
1846 and 1853

August 21, 1853

Dearest Louise,

Have you really not noticed, then, that here of all places, in this private, personal solitude that surrounds me, I have turned to you? All the memories of my youth speak to me as I walk, just as the seashells crunch under my feet on the beach. The crash of every wave awakens far-distant reverberations within me.

I hear the rumble of bygone days and in my mind, the whole endless series of old passions surges forward like the billows. I remember my spasms, my sorrows, gusts of desire that whistled like wind in the rigging and vast vague longings that swirled in the dark like a flock of wild gulls in a storm cloud.

On whom should I lean, if not on you? My weary mind turns for refreshment to the thought of you as a dusty traveler might sink onto a soft and grassy bank.
Gustave

August 15, 1846

I will cover you with love when next I see you, with caresses, with ecstasy. I want to gorge you with all the joys of the flesh so that you faint and die. I want you to be amazed by me and to confess to yourself that you had never even dreamed of such transports... When you are old, I want you to recall those few hours; I want your dry bones to quiver with joy when you think of them.

Adieu, I seal my letter. This is the hour when, alone amidst everything that sleeps, I open the drawer that holds my treasures. I look at your slippers, your handkerchief, your hair, your portrait. I re-read your letters and breathe their musky perfume.
If you could know what I am feeling at this moment! My heart expands in the night, penetrated by a dew of love!

Gustave

August 9, 1846

Dearest Colet,

I embrace you; I kiss you; I feel wild. Were you here, I'd bite you; I long to do so. I, whom, women jeer at for my coldness—I, charitably supposed to be incapable of sex, so little have I indulged in it.

Yet, I feel within me now the appetites of wild beasts, the instincts of a love that is carnivorous, capable of tearing flesh to pieces. Is this love?

Perhaps it is the opposite. Perhaps in my case, it's the heart that is impotent.

Gustave

Nathaniel Hawthorne
To his wife, Sophia Amelia Peabody

5 December 1839

Dearest,

I wish I had the gift of making rhymes, for me thinks there is poetry in my head and heart since I have been in love with you. You are a Poem. Of what sort, then? Epic? Mercy on me, no! A sonnet? No; for that is too labored and artificial. You are a sort of sweet, simple, gay, pathetic ballad, which Nature is singing, sometimes with tears, sometimes with smiles, and sometimes with intermingled smiles and tears.

Sophia Amelia Peabody
To her husband, Nathaniel Hawthorne

December 31, 1839

Best Beloved,

I send you some allumettes wherewith to kindle the taper. There are very few but my second finger could no longer perform extra duty. These will serve till the wounded one be healed, however. How beautiful is it to provide even this slightest convenience for you, dearest! I cannot tell you how much I love you, in this back-handed style.

My love is not in this attitude—it rather bends forward to meet you.

What a year has been to us! My definition of Beauty is that it is love and, therefore, includes both truth and good. But those only who love as we do can feel the significance and force of this.

My ideas will not flow in these crooked strokes. God be with you. I am very well and have walked far in Danvers this cold morning. I am full of the glory of the day.

God bless you, this night of the old year. It has proved the year of our nativity. Ha, not the old earth passed away from us? Are not all things new?

Your Sophie

Lyman Hodge
To his fiancé, Mary Granger
February 10, 1867

Dearest Mary,

...and now love, you with the warm heart and loving eyes whose picture I kissed last night and whose lips I so often kiss in my dreams

whose love enriches me so bountifully with all pleasant memories and sweet anticipations, whose encircling arms shield me from so much evil and harm

whose caresses are so dear and so longed for, awake and in slumber, making my heart beat faster, my flesh tremble, and my brain giddy with delight

whose feet I kiss and whose knees I embrace as a devotee kisses and embraces those of his idol—my darling whose home is in my arms and whose resting place my bosom

who first came to them as a frightened bird but now loves to linger there till long after the midnight chimes have uttered their warning

my life, with your generous soul, my heart's keeper and my true lover

good night: a good night and a fair one to thy sleeping eyes and wearied limb, the precursor of many bright, beautiful mornings when my kisses shall waken thee and my love shall greet thee.

Lyman

Khalil Gibran
On Love

When love beckons to you, follow him,
Though his ways are hard and steep.
And when his wings enfold you yield to him,
Though the sword hidden among his pinions may wound you.

And when he speaks to you believe in him,
Though his voice may shatter your dreams as the north wind
lays waste the garden.

For even as love crowns you so shall he crucify you.
Even as he is for your growth so is he for your pruning.

Even as he ascends to your height and caresses your
tenderest branches that quiver in the sun,
So shall he descend to your roots and shake them in their
clinging to the earth.

Like sheaves of corn he gathers you unto himself.
He threshes you to make you naked.
He sifts you to free you from your husks.
He grinds you to whiteness.
He kneads you until you are pliant;
And then he assigns you to his sacred fire,
that you may become sacred bread for God's sacred feast.

All these things shall love do unto you that you may know the
secrets of your heart, and in that knowledge become a
fragment of Life's heart.

But if in your fear you would seek only love's peace and love's
pleasure,
Then it is better for you that you cover your nakedness and
pass out of love's threshing floor,
Into the seasonless world where you shall laugh, but not all of
your laughter, and weep, but not all of your tears.

Love gives naught but itself and takes naught but from itself.
Love possesses not nor would it be possessed;
For love is sufficient unto love.

When you love you should not say, 'God is in my heart,' but
rather, 'I am in the heart of God.'
And think not you can direct the course of love, for love, if it
finds you worthy, directs your course.

Love has no other desire but to fulfill itself.
But if you love and must needs have desires, let these be your
desires:
To melt and be like a running brook that sings its melody to
the night.
To know the pain of too much tenderness.
To be wounded by your own understanding of love;
And to bleed willingly and joyfully.
To wake at dawn with a winged heart and give thanks for
another day of loving;
To rest at the noon hour and meditate love's ecstasy;
To return home at eventide with gratitude;
And to sleep with a prayer for the beloved in your heart and a
song of praise upon your lips.

Count Gabriel Honore de Mirbeau
To Sophie
1780

Sophie,

To be with the people one loves, says La Bruyere, is enough—
to dream you are speaking to them, not speaking to them,
thinking of them, thinking of the most indifferent things, but
by their side—nothing else matters.

O, mon amie, how true that is! And it is also true that when
one acquires such a habit, it becomes a necessary part of
one's existence.

Alas! I well know, I should know too well since the three
months that I sigh far away from thee, that I possess thee no
more, that my happiness has departed. However, when every
morning I wake up, I look for you—it seems to me that half of
myself is missing—and that is too true.

Twenty times during the day, I ask myself where you are,
judge how strong the illusion is, and how cruel it is to see it
vanish. When I go to bed, I do not fail to make room for you; I
push myself quite close to the wall and leave a great empty
space in my small bed. This movement is mechanical; these
thoughts are involuntary. Ah! How one accustoms oneself to
happiness.

Alas! One only knows it well when one has lost it, and I'm
sure we have only learned to appreciate how necessary we are

LOVE LETTERS OF GREAT MEN

to each other since the thunderbolt has parted us. The source of our tears has not dried up, dear Sophie; we cannot become healed; we have enough in our hearts to love always and, because of that, enough to weep always.

Gabriel

John Keats
To Fanny Brawne
1819-1820

July 1, 1819

My dearest Lady,

...Ask yourself, my love, whether you are very cruel to have so entrammeled me, so destroyed my freedom.

Will you confess this in the letter you must write immediately and do all you can to console me in it—make it rich as a draught of poppies to intoxicate me—write the softest words and kiss them that I may at least touch my lips where yours have been?

For myself, I know not how to express my devotion to so fair a form: I want a brighter word than bright, a fairer word than fair. I almost wish we were butterflies and lived but three summer days—three such days with you I could fill with more delight than fifty common years could ever contain.
But however selfish I may feel, I am sure I could never act selfishly. As I told you a day or two before I left Hampstead, I will never return to London if my fate does not turn up Pam or at least a court-card.

Though I could center my happiness in you, I cannot expect to engross your heart so entirely. Indeed, if I thought you felt as much for me as I do for you at this moment, I do not think

I could restrain myself from seeing you again tomorrow, for the delight of one embrace.

But no—I must live upon hope and chance. In case of the worst that can happen, I shall still love you, but what hatred I shall have for another!

JK

March 1820

Sweetest Fanny,

You fear sometimes I do not love you so much as you wish? My dear girl, I love you ever and ever and without reserve. The more I have known you, the more have I loved. In every way—even my jealousies have been agonies of love; in the hottest fit I ever had I would have died for you.

I have vexed you too much. But for love! Can I help it? You are always new. The last of your kisses was ever the sweetest; the last smile the brightest; the last movement the gracefullest. When you passed my window home yesterday, I was filled with as much admiration as if I had then seen you for the first time. You uttered a half complaint once, that I only loved your beauty.

Have I nothing else then to love in you but that? Do not I see a heart naturally furnished with wings imprison itself with me? No ill prospect has been able to turn your thoughts a moment from me. This, perhaps, should be as much a subject of sorrow as joy. But I will not talk of that.

Even if you did not love me, I could not help an entire devotion to you: how much more deeply, then, must I feel for you knowing you love me.

My mind has been the most discontented and restless one that ever was put into a body too small for it. I never felt my mind repose upon anything with complete and undistracted enjoyment—upon no person but you. When you are in the room, my thoughts never fly out the window; you always concentrate my whole senses.

The anxiety shown about our love, in your last note, is an immense pleasure to me. However, you must not suffer such speculations to molest you any more: not will I any more believe you can have the least pique against me.

Your affectionate,
J. Keats

To Fanny Brawne:

I cannot exist without you. I am forgetful of everything but seeing you again; my life seems to stop there; I see no further. You have absorbed me.
  I have a sensation at the present moment as though I were dissolving ....I have been astonished that men could die martyrs for religion—I have shuddered at it. I shudder no

more. I could be martyred for my religion; love is my religion. I could die for that; I could die for you.

My creed is love and you are its only tenet—you have ravished me away by a power I cannot resist.
 John Keats

Wednesday Morning 1820

My Dearest Girl,

I have been on a walk this morning with a book in my hand, but as usual I have been occupied with nothing but you—I wish I could say, in an agreeable manner. I am tormented day and night. They talk of my going to Italy. It is certain I shall never recover if I am to be so long separate from you. Yet with all this devotion to you, I cannot persuade myself into any confidence of you....

You are to me an object intensely desirable. The air I breathe in a room empty of you is unhealthy. I am not the same to you—no—you can wait. You have a thousand activities—you can be happy without me. Any party, anything to fill up the day has been enough.

How have you passed this month? Who have you smiled with? All this may seem savage in me. You do no feel as I do. You do not know what it is to love. One day you may—your time is not come...

I cannot live without you, and not only you but chaste you,

virtuous you. The sun rises and sets, the day passes, and you follow the bent of your inclination to a certain extent. You have no conception of the quantity of miserable feeling that passes through me in a day.

Be serious! Love is not a plaything. And again, do not write unless you can do it with a crystal conscience. I would sooner die for want of you than...

Yours forever,

J. Keats

Robert Herrick
"Delight In Disorder"

A sweet disorder in the dress
Kindles in clothes a wantonness;
A lawn about the shoulders thrown,
Into a fine distraction,
An erring lace, which here and there
Enthralls the Crimson stomacher,
A cuff neglectful, and thereby
Ribands to flow confusedly,
A winning wave, deserving note,
In the tempestuous petticoat,
A careless shoe-string, in whose tie
I see a wild civility,
Do more bewitch me than when art
is too precise in every part.

Henry IV
To Gabrielle d'Estres
June 16, 1593

From the Battlefield

Gabrielle,

I have waited patiently for one whole day without news of you; I have been counting the time and that's what it must be. But a second day—I can see no reason for it, unless my servants have grown lazy or been captured by the enemy. For I dare not put the blame on you, my beautiful angel: I am too confident of your affection—which is certainly due to me, for my love was never greater, nor my desire more urgent. That is why I repeat this refrain in all my letters: come, come, come, my dear love.

Honor with your presence the man who, if only he were free, would go a thousand miles to throw himself at your feet and never move from there. As for what is happening here, we have drained the water from the moat, but our cannons are not going to be in place until Friday when, God willing, I will dine in town.

The day after you reach Mantes, my sister will arrive at Anet, where I will have the pleasure of seeing you every day. I am sending you a bouquet of orange blossom that I have just received. I kiss the hands of the Vicomtess if she is there, and of my good friend. And as for you, my dear love, I kiss your feet a million times.

Count Leo Tolstoy
To his fiancé, Valeria Arsenev
November 2, 1856

I already love in you your beauty, but I am only beginning to love in you that which is eternal and ever precious: your heart, your soul.

Beauty one could get to know and fall in love with in one hour and cease to love it as speedily. But the soul, one must learn to know. Believe me, nothing on earth is given without labor—even love, the most beautiful and natural of feelings.

King Henry VIII
To Anne Boleyn
1520 and 1528

1528

My Mistress and Friend,

I and my heart put ourselves in your hands, begging you to recommend us to your good grace and not to let absence lessen your affection. For myself, the pang of absence is already too great, and when I think of the increase of what I must need suffer, it would be well nigh intolerable but for my firm hope of your unchangeable affection...

Henry VIII

1520

Anne,

In debating with myself the contents of your letters, I have been put to a great agony; not knowing how to understand them, whether to my disadvantage, as shown in some places, or to my advantage as in others.

I beseech you now, with all my heart, definitely to let me know your whole mind as to the love between us. For necessity compels me to plague you for a reply, having been for more than a year now, struck by the dart of love and being uncertain either of failure or of finding a place in your heart and affection—which point has certainly kept me for some time from naming you my mistress.

Since if you only love me with an ordinary love, the name is not appropriate to you—seeing that it stands for an uncommon position very remote from the ordinary.

But if it pleases you to do the duty of a true, loyal mistress and friend and to give yourself body and heart to me, who have been, and will be, your very loyal servant (if your rigor does not forbid me), I promise you that not only the name will be due to you, but also to take you as my sole mistress, casting off all others than yourself out of mind and affection and to serve you only—begging you to make me a complete reply to this, my rude letter, as to how far and in what I can trust.

And if it does not please you to reply in writing, to let me know of some place where I can have it by word of mouth— the which place I will seek out with all my heart. No more for fear of wearying you. Written by the hand of him who would willingly remain yours.

Henry VIII

Catherine of Aragon
To her ex-husband, Henry VIII
1535

My Lord and Dear Husband,

I commend me unto you. The hour of my death draweth fast on, and my case being such, the tender love I owe you forceth me, with a few words, to put you in remembrance of the health and safeguard of your soul, which you ought to prefer before all worldly matters, and before the care and tendering of your own body, for the which you have cast me into many miseries and yourself into many cares.

For my part I do pardon you all. Yea, I do wish and devoutly pray God that He will also pardon you.

For the rest, I commend unto you Mary, our daughter, beseeching you to be a good father unto her as I heretofore desired. I entreat you also, on behalf of my maids, to give them marriage-portions, which is not much, they being but three. For all my other servants, I solicit a year's pay more than their due, lest they should be unprovided for. Lastly, do I vow, that mine eyes desire you above all things.

Henry Wadsworth Longfellow
"Afternoon In February"

The day is ending,
The night is descending;
The marsh is frozen,
The river dead.
Through clouds like ashes
The red sun flashes
On village windows
That glimmer red.
The snow recommences;
The buried fences
Mark no longer
The road o'er the plain;
While through the meadows,
Like fearful shadows,
Slowly passes
A funeral train.
The bell is pealing,
And every feeling
Within me responds
To the dismal knell;
Shadows are trailing,
My heart is bewailing
And tolling within
Like a funeral bell.

Franz Liszt
To Countess Marie D'Agoult
1834

Thursday morning

Marie,

My heart overflows with emotion and joy!

I do not know what heavenly languor, what infinite pleasure permeates it and burns me up.

It is as if I had never loved!!! Tell me whence these uncanny disturbances spring, these inexpressible foretastes of delight, these divine tremors of love.
Oh! All this can only spring from you:
sister, angel, woman, Marie!

All this can only be, is surely nothing less than a gentle ray streaming from your fiery soul—or else some secret poignant teardrop which you have long since left in my breast.

My God, my God, never force us apart; take pity on us!
But what am I saying? Forgive my weakness.
How could Thou divide us!

Thou would have nothing but pity for us...No no!

It is not in vain that our flesh and our souls quicken and become immortal through Thy Word, which cries out deep

within us: Father, Father...out Thy hand to us, that our broken
hearts seek their refuge in Thee...O!

We thank, bless, and praise Thee, O God for all that Thou has
given us and all that Thou hast prepared for us....

This is to be—to be!
Franz Liszt

December 1834

Marie! Marie!

Oh let me repeat that name a hundred times,
a thousand times over;
for three days now it has lived within me, oppressed me, set
me afire.

I am not writing to you, no, I am close beside you.
I see you; I hear you...
Eternity in your arms...Heaven, hell; all is within you and
even more than all...

Oh! Leave me free to rave in my delirium.
Mean, cautious, narrow reality is no longer enough for me.

We must live our lives to the full,
our loves, our sorrow...!
Oh! You believe me capable of
self-sacrifice, chastity, temperance,
and piety, do you not?

But let no more be said of this...
it is for you to question, to draw conclusions,
to save me as you see fit.
Let me be mad senseless
since you can do nothing, nothing
at all for me.
It is good for me to speak to you now.
This is to be! To be!!!

Franz

Sara Teasdale
"I Am Not Yours"

I am not yours, not lost in you,
Not lost, although I long to be
Lost as a candle lit at noon,
Lost as a snowflake in the sea.

You love me, and I find you still
A spirit beautiful and bright,
Yet I am I, who long to be
Lost as a light is lost in light.

Oh plunge me deep in love -- put out
My senses, leave me deaf and blind,
Swept by the tempest of your love,
A taper in a rushing wind.

Jack London
To Ann Strunsky
April 3, 1901

Dear Anna:

Did I say that the human might be filed in categories? Well, and if I did, let me qualify—not all humans. You elude me. I cannot place you, cannot grasp you. I may boast that of nine out of ten, under given circumstances, I can forecast their action; that of nine out of ten, by their word or action, I may feel the pulse of their hearts. But of the tenth I despair. It is beyond me. You are that tenth.

Were ever two souls, with dumb lips, more incongruously matched! We may feel in common—surely, we often times do—and when we do not feel in common, yet do we understand; and yet we have no common tongue. Spoken words do not come to us. We are unintelligible. God must laugh at the mummery.

The one gleam of sanity through it all is that we are both large temperamentally, large enough to often understand. True, we often understand but in vague glimmering ways by dim perceptions like ghosts, which, while we doubt, haunt us with their truth. And still I, for one, dare not believe; for you are that tenth which I may not forecast.

Am I unintelligible now? I do not know. I imagine so. I cannot find the common tongue.

Large temperamentally—that is it. It is the one thing that brings us at all in touch. We have, flashed through us—you and I—each a bit of universal; and so we draw together. And yet we are so different.

I smile at you when you grow enthusiastic. It is a forgivable smile—nay, almost an envious smile. I have lived twenty-five years of repression. I learned not to be enthusiastic. It is a hard lesson to forget. I begin to forget, but it is so little. At the best, before I die, I cannot hope to forget all or most. I can exult, now that I am learning, in little things, in other things; but of my things and secret things doubly mine, I cannot, I cannot.

Do I make myself intelligible? Do you hear my voice? I fear not. There are posers. I am the most successful of them all.

Jack

Wolfgang Amadeus Mozart
To his Wife Constance
October 17, 1790

PS. While I was writing the last page, tear after tear fell on the paper. But I must cheer up—catch! An astonishing number of kisses are flying about—the deuce! I see a whole crowd of them! Ha! Ha! I have just caught three—they are delicious!

You can still answer this letter, but you must address your reply to Linz, Poste Restante—that is the safest course. As I do not yet know for certain whether I shall go to Regensburg, I can't tell you anything definite. Just write on the cover that the letter is to be kept until called for.

Adieu, Dearest, most beloved little wife. Take care of your health and don't think of walking into town. Do write and tell me how you like our new quarters.

Adieu. I kiss you millions of times.

W. A. Mozart

George Bernard Shaw
To 'Stella' Beatrice Campbell
February 27, 1913

I want my rapscallionly fellow vagabond.
I want my dark lady. I want my angel.
I want my tempter.
I want my Freia with her apples.
I want the lighter of my seven lamps of beauty, honor,
laughter, music, love, life and immortality ... I want my
inspiration, my folly, my happiness,
my divinity, my madness, my selfishness,
my final sanity and sanctification,
my transfiguration, my purification,
my light across the sea,
my palm across the desert,
my garden of lovely flowers,
my million nameless joys,
my day's wage,
my night's dream,
my darling and
my star...

'Stella' Beatrice Campbell
To George Bernard Shaw

18th November 1912
33 Kensington Square

No more shams—a real love letter this time—then I can breathe freely and perhaps, who knows, begin to sit up and get well...

I haven't said 'kiss me' because life is too short for the kiss my heart calls for... All your words are as idle wind. Look into my eyes for two minutes without speaking if you dare! Where would   be your fifty-four years? And my grandmother's heart? And how many hours would you be late for dinner?

If you give me one kiss and you can only kiss me if I say 'kiss me' and I will never say 'kiss me' because I am a respectable widow and I wouldn't let any man kiss me unless I was sure of the wedding ring...

Stella
(Liza, I mean).

Thomas Otway
To Mrs. Barry
1600's

Mrs. Barry,

Could I see you without passion or be absent from you without pain? I need not beg your pardon, for thus renewing my vows, that I love you more than health or any happiness here or hereafter.

Everything you do is a new charm to me. And though I have languished for seven long tedious years of desire, jealously despairing. Yet every minute I see you, I still discover something new and more bewitching. Consider how I love you; what would I not renounce or enterprise for you?

I must have you mine or I am miserable, and nothing but knowing which shall be the happy hour can make the rest of my years, that are to come, tolerable. Give me a word or two of comfort, or resolve never to look on me more. For I cannot bear a kind look and after it a cruel denial.

This minute my heart aches for you, and if I cannot have a right in yours, I wish it would ache till I could complain to you no longer.

Thomas

D.H. Lawrence
"A Love Song"

Reject me not if I should say to you
I do forget the sounding of your voice,
I do forget your eyes that searching through
The mists perceive our marriage, and rejoice.
Yet, when the apple-blossom opens wide
Under the pallid moonlight's fingering,
I see your blanched face at my breast, and hide
My eyes from diligent work, malingering.
Ah, then, upon my bedroom I do draw
The blind to hide the garden, where the moon
Enjoys the open blossoms as they straw
Their beauty for his taking, boon for boon.
And I do lift my aching arms to you,
And I do lift my anguished, avid breast,
And I do weep for very pain of you,
And fling myself at the doors of sleep, for rest.
And I do toss through the troubled night for you,
Dreaming your yielded mouth is given to mine,
Feeling your strong breast carry me on into
The peace where sleep is stronger even than wine.

Sir Walter Raleigh
To His Wife
1603

Dearest,

You shall now receive, my dear wife, my last words in these, my last lines. My love I send you that you may keep it when I am dead, and my counsel that you may remember it when I am no more.

I would not, by my will, present you with sorrows dear Besse. Let them go to the grave with me and be buried in the dust. And seeing that it is not God's will that I should see you anymore in this life, bear it patiently and with a heart like thy self.

First, I send you all the thanks which my heart can conceive or my words can rehearse for your many travails, and care taken for me, which though they have not taken effect as you wished. Yet my debt to you is not the less, but pay it I never shall in this world.

Secondly, I beseech you for the love you bear me living. Do not hide yourself many days, but by your travails seek to help your miserable fortunes and the right of your poor child. Thy mourning cannot avail me, I am but dust...

Remember your poor child for his father's sake, who chose you and loved you in his happiest times. Get those letters which I wrote to the Lords, wherein I sued for my life; God is my witness it was for you and yours that I desired life, but it is true that I disdained myself for begging of it. For know it that your son is the son of a true man and one who, in his own respect, despises death and all his misshapen and ugly forms.

I cannot write much. God he knows how hardly I steal this time while others sleep, and it is also time that I should separate my thoughts from the world. Beg my dead body, which living was denied thee, and either lay it at Sherburne or in Exeter Church by my Father and Mother. I can say no more. Time and death call me away....

Written with the dying hand of sometimes thy husband, but now, alas, overthrown. Yours that was, but now not my own.

Walter Raleigh

Percy Grainger
To Karen Holten
October 10, 1910

When I close my eyes, I think that you stand in front of me, just as when we are first quite alone after a long separation and have not yet kissed each other, but stand and feel both our breaths and both bodies quietly touching each other, and feel beforehand the kiss coming, and the whole world seems full of cream, jam, and dizziness.

Emily Bronte
"Silent In The House"

Come, the wind may never again
Blow as now it blows for us;
And the stars may never again
shine as now they shine;
Long before October returns,
Seas of blood will have parted us;
And you must crush the love in your heart,
and I the love in mine.

John Ruskin
To Euphemia Gray
1847

December 1847

Dear Effie,

I don't know anything dreadful enough to liken to you. You are like a sweet forest of pleasant glades and whispering branches, where people wander on and on in its playing shadows—they know not how far. And when they come near the centre of it, it is all cold and impenetrable. And when they would fain turn, lo—they are hedged with briars and thorns and cannot escape...

You are like the bright, soft, swelling, lovely fields of a high glacier covered with fresh morning snow—which is heavenly to the eye and soft and winning on the foot. But beneath, there are winding clefts and dark places in its cold, cold ice where men fall and rise not again.

John

December 15, 1847

Ah, Effie -

You have such sad, wicked ways without knowing it—such sweet, silver undertones of innocent voice—that when one hears, one is lost. Such slight, short, inevitable, arrowy glances from under the bent eyelashes—such gentle changes of sunny and shadowy expression about the lovely lips—such desperate ways of doing the most innocent things. Mercy on us to hear you ask anybody "whether they take sugar with their peaches." Don't you recollect my being 'temporarily insane' for all the day afterwards—after hearing you ask such a thing...?

Robert Schumann
To Clara
1838

Clara,

How happy your last letters have made me—those since
Christmas Eve! I should like to call you by all the endearing
epithets, and yet I can find no lovelier word than the simple
word 'dear,' but there is a particular way of saying it. My dear
one, then, I have wept for joy to think that you are mine and
often wonder if I deserve you.

One would think that no one man's heart and brain could
stand all the things that are crowded into one day. Where do
these thousands of thoughts, wishes, sorrows, joys, and
hopes come from? Day in, day out, the procession goes on.
But how light-hearted I was yesterday and the day before!
There shone out of your letters so noble a spirit, such faith,
such a wealth of love!

What would I not do for love of you, my own Clara? The
knights of old were better off; they could go through fire or
slay dragons to win their ladies, but we of today have to
content ourselves with more prosaic methods, such as
smoking fewer cigars and the like. After all, though, we can
love—knights or no knights. And so, as ever, only the times
change, not men's hearts...

You cannot think how your letter has raised and
strengthened me... You are splendid. And I have much more

reason to be proud of you than you of me. I have made up my mind, though, to read all your wishes in your face. Then you will think, even though you don't say it, that your Robert is a really good sort, that he is entirely yours and he loves you more than words can say.

You shall indeed have cause to think so, in the happy future. I still see you as you looked in your little cap that last evening. I still hear you call me du. Clara, I heard nothing of what you said but that du. Don't you remember?

But I see you in many another unforgettable guise. Once, you were in a black dress, going to the theatre with Emilia List; it was during our separation. I know you will not have forgotten; it is vivid with me. Another time, you were walking in the Thomasgasschen, with an umbrella up, and you avoided me in desperation. And yet another time, as you were putting on your hat after a concert, our eyes happened to meet, and yours were full of the old unchanging love.
I picture you in all sorts of ways, as I have seen you since. I did not look at you much, but you charmed me so immeasurably... Ah, I can never praise you enough for yourself or for your love of me, which I don't really deserve.

Robert

Arphra Behn
"The Dream"

All trembling in my arms Aminta lay,
Defending of the bliss I strove to take;
Raising my rapture by her kind delay,
Her force so charming was and weak.

The soft resistance did betray the grant,
While I pressed on the heaven of my desires;
Her rising breasts with nimbler motions pant;
Her dying eyes assume new fires.

Now to the height of languishment she grows,
And still her looks new charms put on;
– Now the last mystery of Love she knows,
We sigh, and kiss: I waked, and all was done.

`Twas but a dream, yet by my heart I knew,
Which still was panting, part of it was true:
Oh how I strove the rest to have believed;
Ashamed and angry to be undeceived!

Sir Richard Steele
To Mary Scurlock
1707

Smith-street
West-minster

Madam,

I lay down last night with your image in my thoughts and
have awaken this morning in the same contemplation. The
pleasing transport, with which I'm delighted, has a sweetness
in it attended with a train of ten thousand soft desires,
anxieties, and cares.

The day arises on my hopes with new brightness; youth,
beauty, and innocence are the charming objects that steal me
from myself and give me joys above the reach of ambition,
pride, or glory. Believe me, Fair One, to throw myself at your
feet is giving me the highest bliss I know of earth.
Oh, hasten ye minutes! Bring on the happy morning wherein
to be ever hers, will make me look down on Thrones!

I am tenderly, passionately, faithfully thine,

Percy Shelley
To Mary Godwin
October 27, 1833

Mary,

Oh my dearest love, why are our pleasures so short and so uninterrupted? How long is this to last? Know you, my best Mary, that I feel myself in your absence almost degraded to the level of the vulgar and impure.

I feel their vacant stiff eyeballs fixed upon me, until I seem to have been infected with a loathsome meaning... to inhale a sickness that subdues me to languor. Oh! Those redeeming eyes of Mary that they might beam upon me before I sleep!

Praise my forbearance, oh beloved one, that I do not rashly fly to you... and at least secure a moment's bliss.

Wherefore should I delay ... do you not long to meet me? All that is exalted and buoyant in my nature urges me towards you... reproaches me with cold delay... laughs at all fear and spurns to dream of prudence!

Why am I not with you? Alas, we must not meet.

Percy

Dante Gabriel Rossetti

"The Kiss"

What smouldering senses in death's sick delay
Or seizure of malign vicissitude
Can rob this body of honour, or denude
This soul of wedding-raiment worn to-day?

For lo! even now my lady's lips did play
With these my lips such consonant interlude
As laurelled Orpheus longed for when he wooed
The half-drawn hungering face with that last lay.

I was a child beneath her touch, - a man
When breast to breast we clung, even I and she, -
A spirit when her spirit looked through me, -
A god when all our life-breath met to fan
Our life-blood, till love's emulous ardours ran,
Fire within fire, desire in deity.

Arout Voltaire
To Olympe Dunover
1713

The Hague 1713

Dear Olympe,

I am a prisoner here in the name of the King; they can take my life but not the love that I feel for you. Yes, my adorable mistress, tonight I shall see you if I have to put my head on the block to do it.

For heaven's sake, do not speak to me in such disastrous terms as you write; you must live and be cautious; beware of Madame your mother as of your worst enemy. What do I say? Beware of everybody; trust no one; keep yourself in readiness as soon as the moon is visible; I shall leave the hotel incognito, take a carriage or a chaise. We shall drive like the wind to Sheveningen; I shall take paper and ink with me; we shall write our letters.

If you love me, reassure yourself and call all your strength and presence of mind to your aid; do not let your mother notice anything. Try to have your pictures and be assured that the menace of the greatest tortures will not prevent me to serve you. No, nothing has the power to part me from you; our love is based upon virtue and will last as long as our lives.

Adieu, there is nothing that I will not brave for your sake; you deserve much more than that. Adieu, my dear heart!

Arout Voltaire

Henry von Kleist
To Henriette (Adolfine)
1810

My golden child, my pearl, my precious stone, my crown, my queen and empress. You dear darling of my heart, my highest and most precious, my all and everything, my wife, the baptism of my children, my tragic play, my posthumous reputation. Ach!

You are my second better self, my virtues, my merits, my hope, the forgiveness of my sins, my future sanctity, O little daughter of heaven, my child of God, my intercessor, my guardian angel, my cherubim and seraph, how I love you!

Henry von Kleist

Woodrow Wilson
To his wife Edith Galt

The White House
September 19, 1915

My noble, incomparable Edith,

I do not know how to express or analyze the conflicting emotions that have surged like a storm through my heart all night long. I only know that, first and foremost, in all my thoughts has been the glorious confirmation you gave me last night—without effort, unconsciously, as of course—of all I have ever thought of your mind and heart.

You have the greatest soul, the noblest nature, the sweetest, most loving heart I have ever known. And my love, my reverence, my admiration for you—you have increased in one evening as I should have thought only a lifetime of intimate, loving association could have increased them.

You are more wonderful and lovely in my eyes than you ever were before; and my pride and joy and gratitude that you should love me with such a perfect love are beyond all expression, except in some great poem which I cannot write.

Your own,
Woodrow

Sullivan Ballou
To Sarah
July 14, 1861

My very dear Sarah:

The indications are very strong that we shall move in a few days, perhaps tomorrow. Lest I should not be able to write you again, I feel impelled to write lines that may fall under your eye when I shall be no more.

Our movement may be one of a few days duration and full of pleasure, and it may be one of severe conflict and death to me. Not my will, but thine O God, be done. If it is necessary that I should fall on the battlefield for my country, I am ready. I have no misgivings about, or lack of confidence in, the cause in which I am engaged and my courage does not halt or falter.

I know how strongly American civilization now leans upon the triumph of the government and how great a debt we owe to those who went before us through the blood and suffering of the Revolution. And I am willing—perfectly willing—to lay down all my joys in this life to help maintain this government and to pay that debt.

But, my dear wife, when I know that with my own joys, I lay down nearly all of yours and replace them in this life with cares and sorrows. When, after having eaten for long years the bitter fruit of orphanage myself, I must offer it as their only sustenance to my dear little children. Is it weak or dishonorable, while the banner of my purpose floats calmly and proudly in the breeze, that my unbounded love for you, my darling wife and children, should struggle in fierce, though useless, contest with my love of country?

I cannot describe to you my feelings on this calm summer night when two thousand men are sleeping around me, many of them enjoying the last, perhaps, before that of death—and I, suspicious that death is creeping behind me with his fatal dart, am communing with God, my country, and thee.

I have sought most closely and diligently, and often in my breast, for a wrong motive in thus hazarding the happiness of those I loved, and I could not find one. A pure love of my country and of the principles have often advocated before the people and, "the name of honor that I love more than I fear death," have called upon me, and I have obeyed.

Sarah, my love for you is deathless. It seems to bind me to you with mighty cables that nothing but omnipotence could break; and yet my love of country comes over me like a strong wind and bears me irresistibly on, with all these chains to the battlefield.

The memories of the blissful moments I have spent with you come creeping over me, and I feel most gratified to God and to you that I have enjoyed them so long. And hard it is for me to give them up and burn to ashes the hopes of future years, when God willing, we might still have lived and loved together and seen our sons grow up to honorable manhood around us.

I have, I know, but few and small claims upon Divine Providence, but something whispers to me—perhaps it is the wafted prayer of my little Edgar—that I shall return to my loved ones unharmed. If I do not, my dear Sarah, never forget how much I love you. And when my last breath escapes me on the battlefield, it will whisper your name.

Forgive my many faults and the many pains I have caused you. How thoughtless and foolish I have oftentimes been! How gladly would I wash out with my tears every little spot upon your happiness and struggle with all the misfortune of this world to shield you and my children from harm. But I cannot. I must watch you from the spirit land and hover near you, while you buffet the storms with your precious little freight and wait with sad patience till we meet to part no more.

But, O Sarah! If the dead can come back to this earth and flit unseen around those they loved, I shall always be near you; in the garish day and in the darkest night—amidst your happiest scenes and gloomiest hours—always, always; and if there be a soft breeze upon your cheek, it shall be my breath; or the cool air fans your throbbing temple, it shall be my spirit passing by.

Sarah, do not mourn me dead; think I am gone and wait for thee, for we shall meet again.

As for my little boys, they will grow as I have done, and never know a father's love and care. Little Willie is too young to remember me long, and my blue-eyed Edgar will keep my frolics with him among the dimmest memories of his childhood. Sarah, I have unlimited confidence in your maternal care and your development of their characters. Tell my two mothers, his and hers, I call God's blessing upon them. O, Sarah, I wait for you there! Come to me, and lead thither my children.

Sullivan

Edgar Allen Poe
To Frances S. Osgood
1845

Thou wouldst be loved?--then let thy heart
   From its present pathway part not;
Being everything which now thou art,
   Be nothing which thou art not.
So with the world thy gentle ways,
   Thy grace, thy more than beauty,
Shall be an endless theme of praise.
   And love a simple duty.

Alexander Hamilton
To his wife
August 1781

My dear wife,

In my last letter, I informed you that there was a greater prospect of activity now than there had been before. I did this to prepare your mind for an event, which, I am sure, will give you pain. I begged your father at the same time to intimate to you, by degrees, the probability of its taking place. I used this method to prevent a surprise which might be too severe to you.

A part of the army, my dear girl, is going to Virginia and I must, of necessity, be separated at a much greater distance from my beloved wife. I cannot announce the fatal necessity without feeling everything that a fond husband can feel. I am unhappy beyond expression. I am unhappy because I am to be so remote from you; because I am to hear from you less frequently than I am accustomed to do.

I am miserable because I know you will be so; I am wretched at the idea of flying so far from you, without a single hour's interview, to tell you all my pains and all my love. But I cannot ask permission to visit you.

It might be thought improper to leave my corps at such a time and upon such an occasion. I must go without seeing you; I must go without embracing you; alas! I must go. But let no idea, other than of the distance we shall be asunder, disquiet you.

Though I said the prospects of activity will be greater, I said it to give your expectations a different turn and prepare you for something disagreeable. It is ten to one that our views will be disappointed by Cornwallis, retiring to South Carolina by land. At all events, our operations will be over by the latter end of October, and I will fly to my home. Don't mention I am going to Virginia.

Alexander

Index

CPSIA information can be obtained at www.ICGtesting.com
Printed in the USA
239508LV00004B/611/P